True Democracy - A New System Of Government For The World

by -- Maze

This edition is dedicated to the world and you the reader.

Yours truly

Maze

Table of Contents

Preface

How this book came about?

When I was in college, I was constantly debating with my friends and colleagues all the issues the citizens of the country faced and also the issues faced by citizens of other countries in the world. We were debating whether parliamentary democracy was suited to our country where almost nothing got done, and if it did, it was extremely tedious and took a long time. By the way, that country is India and this was in the 90s. I tried to analyse in my head, which system of government is the best. At one point I have considered monarchy and dictatorship to be a good system, provided the monarch was good, cared about the welfare of the people (which is utmost in his/her mind), was a good administrator and an economist. We even considered communism as laid down by Marx, but in reality not practised by any nation in history *(note: the governments of former USSR, China, North Korea, etc. are actually dictatorships, and only communism in name and at times when it comes to economic functions)*. We also discussed about how corruption is a major issue in every nation.

I slowly began to realize that all the problems such as corruption, rioting, etc. were just symptoms of the flawed systems of government existing today and at any time in history. I also realized that these symptoms turned up because in every existing system of government practised by nations the rulers or decision makers were not accountable to the people. Even in a democracy the decision makers are not accountable. The people have to wait for their term to pass and the next elections before they can be removed from office by being voted out, and then again these people cannot be prosecuted for misgovernment because mechanisms have been put in place to shield and protect them.

I was also against all the wars being fought between nations and desired a single system of government for the entire world. Also, why shouldn't every person, whether in the Middle East, Africa, Asia, etc. enjoy the same freedom, liberties and standard of living that people in the west enjoy.

I was also against the blind practice and preaching of religion of any kind, and religion playing an important role in the decision-making of many governments including the so-called secular ones.

I also long came to the conclusion that all religions are man-made. For one, if there was a God and he is all that every religion says about him, such as humble, omnipotent, all-knowing, without any ego, etc., then why would this God require people to believe in him, let alone demand worship and submission. Only a being that has a big ego, such as man, demands worship and submission. Again, ego is an evil trait. Also, by saying all unbelievers will be banished to hell, is implying that God is vengeful. Again this is a human trait and it is evil. By saying all this you not only insult this God, but you are also calling him evil. A final point I would like to clarify, if this God wanted to pass a message to the people why would he require so-called prophets to do so, couldn't he reveal the message himself, after all he is the all-knowing, omnipotent creator.

After analysing all this, I decided that the solution lay in designing a new system of government and administration for the entire world where the people really did have an equal and direct say in all decision-making processes and every individual had an equal share in the revenue generated and utilized by the administration, and religion played no role in government and administration.

One evening when I was discussing this with a couple of elderly colleagues while sitting outside their house in the countryside, my colleagues suggested that I should put this down on paper, and that is when the book started to take shape.

*Note: What I laid down in this book is a basic framework for government, administration, rights and law & order for a **new and better, truly democratic system of government for the whole world,** where every individual, irrespective of his/her community, region, etc. has an equal say in the decision-making processes and an equal share in revenue utilization.*

How This Book Is Organized

This book has been organized into 11 parts or chapters.

1. **Flaws with existing/prevailing systems of government & world order.**
   It briefly lists the existing/prevailing systems of government and the case for a single unified system of world government and order based on an equal distribution of population between various levels of world divisions or administrative units such as nations, states, districts, etc..

2. **A truly democratic system of world government & administrative structure.**
   It gives the framework for dividing the world into various administrative levels/units and a system of government where every individual has an equal and direct say in all decision-making processes.

3. **Administration in the new system of world government.**

It talks about the role played by the administrations of the various administrative units.

4. **World economy, revenue collection and revenue distribution/utilization.**

It briefly talks about a single currency world economy and the process of government revenue collection and revenue distribution/utilization where every individual has an equal share in government revenue utilization.

5. **Arthakranti Proposal.**

It talks about a Government Revenue or Taxation System as proposed by the "Arthakranti Sansthan" which is an Economic Advisory body constituted by a group of Chartered Accountants and Engineers in Pune, India.

6. **Law & rights in a truly democratic system of world government.**

It talks about universal law & set of rights which will apply to every individual equally.

7. **The justice system & the administering of justice.**

It briefly describes the justice system and how justice will be administered.

8. **Enforcement of law & order and protecting the world.**

It talks about the law & order enforcing mechanisms and agencies involved in the same.

9. **Law governing land ownership.**

It talks about the law governing ownership and sale of land and the distribution of revenue from sale of land by the government.

10. **Law governing corporates.**

It briefly explains how corporations will be governed.

11. **Conclusion.**

It contains the final concluding thoughts.

Flaws With Existing/Prevailing Systems Of Government & World Order

Government run by a religious Body

1. The government is run by a body of religious clerics who are not elected and are not accountable. The head of this body has absolute power and may even be thought of as a dictator.

2. The government and administration of law & order is based on laws laid down in texts (known as scripture) written hundreds and even thousands of years ago in ancient times when tribal culture existed. These laws are not only outdated and barbaric, they even restrict individual freedoms and human rights.

Monarchy & dictatorships

1. The government is run on the whims of one person. Even if he/she is a genuinely good person with good intentions for the welfare of his/her nation's citizens, he/she is born with human frailties, such as ego, irrational emotions, etc. which could result in decisions that could go against the welfare of citizens. His/her ego could prevent him/her from taking sane advice from his/her advisers and ministers.

2. The monarch or dictator can never be knowledgeable on the intricacies of governance, etc..

3. Unless the monarch or dictator has done an exhaustive / advance course in economics, he/she is wont to taking poor economic decisions, etc..

Communist governments such as China, Cuba, etc.

1. The government is run by a Single Party headed by an all powerful leader who can also be considered a dictator.

2. Although communism states that there should be collateral decision-making and all should share equally in the fruits and profits of the land, in reality that is not the case. A few people who are part of the government or administration enjoy all the privileges whereas the remaining people have to struggle and at times live in abject poverty. Also, in most cases the leader of the communist party is in charge. So although communism as stated by Karl Marx states that there should be no single person in authority and all decisions should be made in consensus by all the people of the nation, in reality what is practised is quite the opposite and the people have no say in any decision-making.

3. The biggest flaw of communism is mediocrity and merit going unrecognised and unrewarded leading to complacency. This

leads to lack of growth and progress and even leads to negative growth or decline in economy. The best argument for this was given by a classroom teacher. When there was an argument made by a student or 2 against free market, he decided to create an experiment to show the flaws in communism and virtues of the free market. He said from today every student will get equal marks or grades for their performance, which will be the average or mean of the marks the students of the class achieved. So the next time their papers were graded every student received 70%. All the low performing students became really happy and they started to work even less hard on their tests. And gradually the average or mean marks fell even more and came down to 60%. Slowly the top performing students started to feel disgruntled and felt let down by the others since the low performers were dragging their grades down as well, and they thought to themselves why should we work harder and harder and our grades falling when the others kept getting more and more complacent. So the top performers too stopped working hard and soon the average or mean grades fell really low, 40% and below. Soon a blame game began and finally they decided to go back to the old grading system.

4. Finally, as an information gathering mechanism and reader of what people want and what they are willing to pay for it, the free market system works better than even the most powerful computer ever designed. It is able to correctly relay information about prices, supply and demand in real time, without any contraption costing billions of dollars being put in place for the purpose. Also, manufacturers are able to quickly realize what people want and what works and how much of their earnings they wish to sacrifice to obtain it, therefore they will stop wasting resources manufacturing products that people don't want or need or manufacturing products at a cost that people are not willing to pay. Free market also leads to production efficiency and reduction in unit cost of manufacturing a product through economies of scale, without any wasteful over-production.

Existing so-called democratic systems in UK, USA, India, etc.

There exists mainly 2 types of democratic systems.

A) Parliamentary democracy (such as in India, UK, etc.) where people elect representatives to the parliament for a fixed term and the representatives belonging to the majority political party or a coalition of political parties form the government.

B) Presidential Democracy (such as in USA, France, etc.) where the people elect both the representatives to the senate or parliament and the president who becomes the chief executive and head of state for a fixed term.

Below is listed the generic flaws of both these systems.

1. System was created by the British at around 1400 AD or 1500 AD onwards. The conditions that prevailed then were different. Also, population per constituency was much lower compared to today's population per constituency.

2. When it was designed, it was designed mainly for the elites and it still retains some of those elitist features. Members of parliament and state assemblies today roam around in security escorted cars (*at least in India*). They are not easily approachable by the common man. They entitle themselves to various perks and salaries, which the average man can only dream of. The members of parliament and state legislative assemblies behave like they are untouchable or gods.

3. The system is extremely bureaucratic. The bureaucracy still controls most of the administration. Even though most decisions are made by cabinet of ministers appointed by winning party, these decisions are mainly based on suggestions and options laid down by the bureaucracy, so despite it seeming that the ministers are in control it is actually the bureaucracy that controls everything. This bureaucracy is uncontrollable since bureaucrats are not appointed by the people and laws have been made so that bureaucrats cannot be easily prosecuted or removed from

office despite wrongdoing or misconduct or lack of performance.

4. The representatives are not accountable to the people until the next elections. And even then laws have been made to shield them from any punishment or conviction that can be meted out to them. Despite there being different political parties, these parties are hand in glove since they know if one MP is framed he/she shall spill the beans on the others.

5. Most of the members of parliament are under control of the party head or functionaries. Therefore they do not truly represent their constituencies, but their parties.

6. Even from an electoral point of view the Member of Parliament (MP) does not represent the people. For example an average constituency of around 500000 to 1 million people in India. Of these only 70% are registered voters. Of these only 60% vote (60% of 70 is approx. 40%) so 40% of the total population. Now if there are 3 candidates and all 3 receive an equal number of votes, but 1

candidate receives just 1 vote more than the other 2 then he/she gets approx. 1/3rd of the votes and wins (1/3rd of 40 is approx. 13) so only 13% of the population votes for the winning candidate and 87% did not vote for him/her. How can we say that this candidate represents all the people of the constituency.

7. The election process in many countries results in wasteful amount of expenditure that could be better utilized for healthcare, education, utilities, etc. for the welfare of the people. Also, in many countries elections are a farce with many people not inclined to vote. There is vote rigging, buying of votes, etc.. It also comes in the way of economic activities due to election day being declared a holiday.

8. The system is extremely complicated, inefficient and wasteful.

9. A large portion of revenue collected goes to pay for central projects and other expenses which does not benefit the locality a person lives in even though it is that person who pays the taxes *(70% of tax paid by a person should directly go to the locality a person lives in)*. In

fact, in India most of the revenue indirectly ends up in politicians & bureaucrats pockets through corruption.

10.   The biggest flaw is that the existing system has a top down approach reminiscent of the old monarchical system. A top down approach is a centralized system and is extremely dictatorial, inefficient and wasteful. It is very difficult to check whether funds reach the designated people or projects in a top down approach. It is also extremely corruptible. Also, it is very difficult to implement decisions and get information passed to all levels correctly. Flow of information is very inefficient in a top down approach. Decision-making and law enforcement also becomes very complicated. Whereas in a bottom up approach everything is decentralized and simplified, there is no inefficiency or wastage and it is very easy to check if the decision and information reaches the top since no parallel branches are involved and it is a straight up process.

Flaws with existing world order

1. The existing organization of the world into nations give a disproportionate say to people in world affairs. For example, the vote of a nation with a population of few 100000 such as Mauritius, Granada, Vanuatu, Maldives, Seychelles in the United nations world body holds the same weightage as the vote of a nation having a population of a Billion or more such as India. This shows that the voice of 100000 people carries the same weightage as the voice of a Billion people. Therefore if you divide the vote by the population of the nation you will see that each individual in the first nation of 100000 has a greater say compared to each individual in the 2nd nation of a Billion people. Also, the vote of a nation which belongs to the 6 permanent members of security council having veto power carries a greater weightage *(due to the veto power)* than the nation having population 10 times some of these nations. This is inequality on a grand scale.

2. The share of the world's natural resources (which are not created by anyone) is also

disproportionate to the population of the nations. Some rich nations with far less population have a far greater share in earth's natural resources than other nations with larger populations. *Note: One nation even holds the greatest amount of debt far exceeding any nation on earth (The USA) and their people enjoy more fruits and a higher standard of living than some nations who have zero debts or whose balance of payments is in the positive, such as China, Japan, etc.. And yet the currency of this nation carries greater weightage than the currency of the other 2 nations. This nation is living off the hard work and labour of the citizens of the other nations.*

3. The freedom, liberty, rights and welfare enjoyed by people living in the west is denied to majority of people in the world. Don't these people deserve the same freedom, liberties, rights and welfare.

4. Finally, the existing organization of the world into nations, provinces, etc. with concepts of nationalism, provincialism, religion, tribe, language, culture, etc. robs an individual of

his/her identity   and of his/her self distinct from religion, tribe, community, nation, etc.. It also results in conflicts and wars waged on the basis of nationalism, religion, culture, tribe, etc..

A Truly Democratic System Of World Government & Administrative Structure

Why do academicians, journalists, administrators, governments of the so-called democratic nations (India, USA, UK, etc.) call themselves democracies when they do not practice democracy in the true sense of the term. Below is how a truly democratic system of government for the world should function:

Organization of the world into various administrative levels/units and their government structure

Constituency/locality (the smallest administrative unit) government

The whole world should be divided into constituencies/localities *(which will be the smallest administrative unit)* of 600 to 900 people each *(approx 200 families)*. Each constituency/locality should elect a committee and chairman to govern

28

the constituency/locality *(usually through a simple majority consensus of all the residents of the constituency/locality above the age of 18 years)*. The committee members and chairman can be replaced any time through majority consensus of the residents *(above the age of 18 years)* of the constituency/locality. The chairman coordinates the activities of the committee and if there is a stalemate or no consensus then he/she has the final say. All major decisions taken by the committee require consent/sanction of majority residents of the constituency/locality *(above 18 years of age)*.

Town government

A group of constituencies/localities will constitute a town. Every town should be made up of equal number of constituencies/localities *(as far as possible the constituencies/localities will be divided equally into towns)*. The constituencies/localities will each appoint a representative to represent the constituency/locality in the town assembly. This appointment will be done by the committee of the constituency/locality and will require consent of majority residents of the constituency/locality *(above 18 years of age)*. This representative can be replaced any time by the committee of the constituency/locality he/she represents. This representative will be the voice of the constituency/locality in the town assembly. Any bills the constituency/locality needs to introduce in the town assembly will be done through him/her. All bills introduced by this representative or voting done by this representative in the town assembly requires consent/sanction of the committee and majority residents of the constituency/locality he/she represents.

The town assembly appoints a town cabinet of ministers and town mayor to administer the town. Since they are appointed, they can be replaced any time and are answerable to the town assembly. The town mayor is there to only coordinate the activities of the ministers and in case there is no consensus among the ministers or the members of the assembly then he/she will have the final say. He/she also makes sure the town administration does not interfere in the administration of a constituency/locality. However, he/she will not have any other decision-making powers.

Sub-district government

A group of towns will constitute a sub-district. Every sub-district should have equal number of towns *(as far as possible the towns will be divided equally into sub-districts)*. The towns will each appoint a representative to represent the town in the sub-district assembly. This appointment will be done by the town assembly and will require the consent of majority assembly members. This representative can be replaced any time by the town assembly. This representative will be the voice of the town in the sub-district assembly. Any bills the town needs to introduce in the sub-district assembly will be done through him/her. All bills introduced by this representative or voting done by this representative in the sub-district assembly requires consent/sanction of the majority members of the town assembly he/she represents.

The Sub-district assembly appoints a sub-district cabinet of ministers and sub-district mayor to administer the sub-district. Since they are appointed, they can be replaced any time and are answerable to the sub-district assembly. The sub-district mayor is there to only coordinate the activities of the ministers and in case there is no

31

consensus among the ministers or the members of the assembly then he/she will have the final say. He/she also makes sure the sub-district administration does not interfere in the administration of a town or constituency/locality. However, he/she will not have any other decision-making powers.

District government

A group of sub-districts will constitute a district. Every district should have equal number of sub-districts *(as far as possible the sub-districts will be divided equally into districts)*. The sub-districts will each appoint a representative to represent the sub-district in the district assembly. This appointment will be done by the sub-district assembly and will require the consent of majority assembly members. This representative can be replaced any time. This representative will be the voice of the sub-district in the district assembly. Any bills the sub-district needs to introduce in the district assembly will be done through him/her. All bills introduced by this representative or voting done by this representative in the district assembly requires consent/sanction of the majority members of the sub-district assembly he/she represents.

The district assembly appoints a district cabinet of ministers and district mayor to administer the district. Since they are appointed, they can be replaced any time and are answerable to the district assembly. The district mayor is there to only coordinate the activities of the ministers and in case there is no consensus among the ministers or the members of the assembly then he/she will have the final say. He/she also makes sure the district administration does not interfere in the administration of a Sub-district or town or constituency/locality. However, he/she will not have any other decision-making powers.

State government

A group of districts will constitute a state. Every state should have equal number of districts *(as far as possible the districts will be divided equally into states)*. The districts will each appoint a representative to represent the district in the state assembly. This appointment will be done by the district assembly and will require the consent of majority assembly members. This representative can be replaced any time. This representative will be the voice of the district in the state assembly. Any bills the district needs to introduce in the state assembly will be done through him/her. All bills introduced by this representative or voting done by this representative in the state assembly requires consent/sanction of the majority members of the district assembly he/she represents.

The state assembly appoints a state cabinet of ministers and state governor to administer the state. Since they are appointed, they can be replaced any time and are answerable to the state assembly. The state governor is there to only coordinate the activities of the ministers and in case there is no consensus among the ministers or the members of the assembly then he/she will have the final say. He/she also makes sure the state administration does not interfere in the administration of a district or sub-district or town or constituency/locality. However, he/she will not have any other decision-making powers.

National government

A group of states will constitute a nation. Every nation should have equal number of states *(as far as possible the states will be divided equally into nations)*. The states will each appoint a representative to represent the state in the national assembly. This appointment will be done by the state assembly and will require the consent of majority assembly members. This representative can be replaced any time. This representative will be the voice of the state in the national assembly. Any bills the state needs to introduce in the national assembly will be done through him/her. All bills introduced by this representative or voting done by this representative in the national assembly requires consent/sanction of the majority members of the state assembly he/she represents.

The national assembly appoints a national cabinet of ministers and a prime minister to administer the nation. Since they are appointed, they can be replaced any time and are answerable to the national assembly. The prime minister is there to only coordinate the activities of the ministers in the national cabinet and in case there is no consensus among the ministers or members of the national assembly then he/she will have the final say. He/she also makes sure the national administration does not interfere in the administration of a state or district or sub-district or town or constituency/locality. However, he/she will not have any other decision-making powers.

World government

The national assemblies each appoint a representative to represent the nation in the world assembly, and he/she can be replaced any time. This representative will be the voice of the nation in the world assembly. Any bills the nation needs to introduce in the world assembly will be done through him/her. All bills introduced by this representative or voting done by this representative in the world assembly requires consent/sanction of the majority members of the national assembly he/she represents.

The world assembly appoints a world cabinet of ministers and a president to administer the world. Since they are appointed, they can be replaced any time and are answerable to the world assembly. The president is there to only coordinate the activities of the ministers in the world cabinet and in case there is no consensus among the ministers or members of the world assembly then he/she will have the final say. He/she also makes sure the world administration does not interfere in the administration of a nation or state or district or sub-district or town or constituency/locality. However, he/she will not have any other decision-making powers.

Note: The above organization and division of the world into administrative units of localities / towns / sub-districts / districts / states/ nations is for administrative/government purposes only. By dividing administration/government into the various levels stated above, administration becomes easy and more manageable. Also, since representatives and ministers can be replaced any time and their actions require consent of the people who appointed them, it makes them accountable and enables better control of government by the people at all levels through a bottom up approach where people at the bottom control people at the top and all decisions and information flow from the bottom to the top. This bottom up approach enables decisions and information to easily reach the concerned level since no parallel branches are involved. Since all decisions are taken through simple majority consensus/vote by representatives in the various assemblies when it comes to town / sub-district / district / state / national / world administration, or simple majority consensus/vote of residents of constituency/locality when it comes to constituency/locality administration, there is no need for large scale elections that result in wasteful expenditure. It also makes sure that the number of people voting at every level is small and more manageable and thus no need for huge elections, etc.. Also, by making sure that the world administration only involves resolving conflicts between 2 or more nations, national administration only involves resolving conflicts between states within it, state administration only involves resolving conflicts between 2 or more districts within it and so on ..., the task or work of the various administrative units is reduced and made more manageable.

By distributing the people equally among the various constituencies/localities, towns, sub-districts, districts, states and nations you make sure that every individual has an equal say in the decision process at all levels.

Re-organization of the world when there is a change in population

Every individual will have a residency status which mentions which locality he/she permanently resides in. When an individual moves to another locality permanently, he/she is required to have his/her/its residency status changed. Every individual has the freedom and right to move to any locality in any town, sub-district, district, state, nation or the world unless he/she/it is incarcerated for breaking a law.

If the population of a constituency/locality becomes >= 1200 or 1500 (>= 400 families) then the constituency/locality should be split into 2. And if the population falls below a minimum threshold (< 200) or (< 50 families) then it should be merged with an adjacent constituency/locality.

If the number of constituencies/localities in a town increase or decrease, the constituencies/localities should be redistributed or if necessary new towns should be formed.

If the number of towns in a sub-district increase or decrease, the towns should be redistributed among various sub-districts and if necessary new sub-districts should be formed.

If the number of sub-districts in a district increase or decrease the sub-districts should be redistributed among various districts and if necessary new districts should be formed.

If the number of districts in a state increase or decrease then the districts should be redistributed among various states and if necessary new states should be formed.

If the number of states in a nation increase or decrease then the states should be redistributed among various nations and if necessary new nations should be formed.

This will ensure that all the people are properly & equally represented in government at all levels of administration.

A special body will be set up by the world administration and it will be entrusted with the above task.

Note: Depending on the Population of the world, the levels between world administration and constituency/locality may vary. If the population is small, you may only have constituency – town – district – state – nation and world. Here the sub-district can be left out. Or if it becomes too big, you may add one more level between locality and town called town-segment or area. However, the general governing system will remain the same, only the levels in the government/administrative structure will reduce or increase. The size of each constituency/locality may also be reduced or slightly increased to make it more manageable.

Administration In The New System Of World Government

Constituency/locality administration

Each constituency/locality will administer itself through a committee elected by majority residents with no interference from outside.

Town administration

Every town will have an assembly and cabinet of ministers *(as mentioned in the previous chapter)* which will create various administrative bodies as required and appoint officials to administer the town. The town administration will not interfere in the administration of a constituency/locality. It will deal with those matters (such as road work, utilities, setting schools, parks, etc.) which concern/involve 2 or more constituencies/localities of the town and with resolving conflicts between 2 or more constituencies/localities within the town.

Sub-district administration

Every sub-district will have an assembly and cabinet of ministers *(as mentioned in the previous chapter)* which will create various administrative bodies as required and appoint officials to administer the sub-district. The sub-district administration will not interfere in the administration of a town or constituency. It will only deal with those matters, which concern/involve 2 or more towns of the sub-district and with resolving conflicts between 2 or more towns of the sub-district.

District administration

Every district will have an assembly and cabinet of ministers *(as mentioned in the previous chapter)* which will create various administrative bodies as required and appoint officials to administer the district. The district administration will not interfere in the administration of a sub-district or town or constituency/locality. It will only deal with those matters, which concern/involve 2 or more sub-districts of the district and with resolving conflicts between 2 or more sub-districts of the district.

State administration

Every state will have an assembly and cabinet of ministers *(as mentioned in the previous chapter)* which will create various administrative bodies as required and appoint officials to administer the state. The state administration will not interfere in the administration of a district or sub-district or town or constituency/locality. It will only deal with those matters, which concern/involve 2 or more districts of the state and with resolving conflicts between 2 or more districts of the state.

National administration

Every nation will have an assembly and cabinet of ministers (as mentioned in the previous chapter) which will create various administrative bodies as required and appoint officials to administer the nation. The national administration will not interfere in the administration of a state or district or sub-district or town or constituency/locality. It will only deal with those matters, which concern/involve 2 or more states of the nation and with resolving conflicts between 2 or more states of the nation.

World administration

The world will have an assembly and cabinet of ministers *(as mentioned in the previous chapter)* which will create various administrative bodies as required and appoint officials to administer the world. The world administration will not interfere in the administration of a nation or state or district or sub-district or town or constituency/locality. It will only deal with those matters, which concern/involve 2 or more nations and with resolving conflicts between 2 or more nations.

Language/s to be used for administration purposes

The official language for world administration will be English which today is the most known language, even though it may not be the most spoken. You go to any place in the world today and you will find someone who knows and understands English. Also, many Non-English speaking nations have English as a second language taught in schools. There are some Non-English speaking nations with a population of a billion, such as India, which have English as the language of instruction for higher studies and also due to many languages prevailing in its different regions English continues to be retained as the language for central administration (*All administrative forms are available in English, Hindi and a local language).* The strongest case for English to be used as the official language for world administration is that it is the dominant language on the internet and the language used in information systems.

In addition to English being the language for world administration, there will also be national / state / district / sub-District / town / locality languages. All administrative forms will be made available in English as well as the official national language, the official state language, the official district language, the official sub-district language, the official town language and the official locality language.

An applicant shall fill the form in any language of his/her choice, and the applicant's details will then be translated and copied into English which will be the official language for world administration. When a form is filled in a language other than English, there will always be 2 copies of the form, 1 will be the original (in the language used by the applicant) and the 2nd will be its English translation copy.

World Economy And Monetary System, Revenue Collection & Revenue Distribution/Utilization

World economy and monetary system

With regards to world economy & monetary system, all existing currencies will be converted into a single currency or medium of exchange known as the world dollar, which will be closely based on the US dollar which is the current international currency. The exchange rates *(closely pegged to the US Dollar)* will be determined by a world body known as the world bank set up by the world administration. Only bank balances held by individuals and organizations shall be converted *(this will make black & unlawful money in the form of physical cash hidden away valueless, but exceptions will be made for very small amounts of physical cash held by poor individuals having no bank accounts).* Any new notes printed shall hold no value. After the currency conversion is completed these currencies shall cease to exist. Also, physical money will cease to exist and there will be no notes,

47

and all transactions will be done through the banking system or through virtual electronic money as mentioned below.

A world bank set up by the world administration, as mentioned above, will maintain virtual or electronic money balances of all individuals and entities *(including government entities such as the world administration and all the national, state, district, sub-district, town & constituency/locality administrations)*. Every individual and entity will have a virtual or electronic money account in this bank and they will be issued cheque/check books and debit cards to carry out day to day monetary transactions *(note: the government entities will not have any debit cards and will only have the facility of cheque/check books & other means for monetary transactions)*. This world bank will also enable electronic money transfer and other virtual or electronic monetary transactions. This bank will have very secure systems in which all possible frauds will be prevented. The bank's systems will be so designed and its security so robust & secure that no individual or entity will be able to commit fraud, hack the system, cheat the system or break it. The job of this bank will be to maintain the virtual money balances of all individuals and entities and enable monetary transactions. The world bank will also strictly monitor other banks which will have accounts in the world bank and will have to register with it to operate. The world bank shall also frame rules for all banks to follow. The world bank will have no other functions and will not carry out any investment or lending activity.

Every unit of product such as cars, wires, equipment, packaged goods, food, livestock etc. newly produced along with their current value/price minus the cost of materials used will have to be registered with the world economic body and accordingly tagged. The process of registration and tagging will be very easy and quick and instantaneous. As determined by the world economic body, the money in all the accounts with the world bank will be increased by the rate calculated as (total value of all new goods produced minus cost of materials used divided by total money in all the accounts with the world bank) every 3 months or a year. This will prevent money hoarding and economic deflation by creating the extra money needed to purchase the new goods.

The above mentioned monetary system will preserve the 2 other functions of money which are 'store of value' & 'measure of value' (besides the function of 'means of exchange') by preventing inflation since no excess money will be created.

Revenue collection

With regards to revenue collection I at first thought of a system where revenue is collected by the constituency/locality in any manner it wants and 30% of revenue collected or 2% - 4% of the GDP of the constituency/locality (*as determined by the world administration*) whichever is higher goes to the town administration. And 30% of revenue received by each town goes to the sub-district administration and so on... till the top world administration. Then one day I read an article about the Arthakranti Proposal *(explained below and in the next chapter)* and found it to be a more efficient & equitable system of government revenue collection.

For government revenue collection, the world should follow the Arthakranti Proposal which is further explained in the next chapter. All notes should be recalled and scrapped. All cash transactions should be disallowed (we can do away with paper or hard currency altogether). All transactions will be either electronic (debit & credit cards) or online (web transactions) or via cheque/check. These are all banking transactions. A world bank set up by the world administration, as mentioned above, shall maintain virtual or electronic money balances of all individuals and entities and enable virtual or electronic money transactions through system of cheque/check books, debit cards, electronic money transfer and other such systems. Now as per the <u>Arthakranti Proposal,</u> for government revenue collection introduce single point tax system through banking system (including world bank system) known as Banking Transaction Tax (2% to 0.7%) on only credit amount. This amount will be automatically deducted or debited from the amount credited into an individual's or entity's bank account (*including his/her/its world bank account)* and transferred or credited to the world administration's account in the world bank.

Revenue distribution/utilization

With regards to revenue distribution/utilization, 20% to 30% of all revenue collected through the above mentioned system will go to the world administration and remaining 70% to 80% will be divided equally among the nations *(the system of revenue division will be automated, i.e. 20% to 30% will be credited into the world administration's account and the remaining will be credited to the accounts of all the nations equally).*

From the revenue received by the nation from the world administration, 20% to 30% will be kept by the national administration and remaining 70% to 80% will be distributed equally among the states of the nation *(this will be automated - from the revenue credited to the nation's account 70% to 80% will be automatically debited and credited into the accounts of all states within the nation equally).*

From the revenue received by the state from the national administration, 20% to 30% will be kept by the state administration and remaining 70% to 80% will be distributed equally among the districts of the state *(this will be automated - from the revenue credited to the state's account 70% to 80% will be automatically debited and credited into the accounts of all districts within the state equally).*

From the revenue received by the district from the state, 20% to 30% will be kept by the district administration and remaining 70% to 80% will be distributed equally among the Sub-districts of the district *(this will be automated - from the revenue credited to the district's account 70% to 80% will be automatically debited and credited into the accounts of all Sub-districts within the district equally).*

From the revenue received by the sub-district from the district, 20% to 30% will be kept by the sub-district administration and remaining 70% to 80% will be distributed equally among the towns of the sub-district *(this will be automated - from the revenue credited to the sub-district's account 70% to 80% will be automatically debited and credited into the accounts of all towns within the sub-district equally).*

From the revenue received by the town from the sub-district, 20% to 30% will be kept by the town administration and remaining 70% to 80% will be distributed equally among the constituencies/localities of the town *(this will be automated - from the revenue credited to the town's account 70% to 80% will be automatically debited and credited into the accounts of all constituencies/localities within the town equally).*

Note: The above mentioned system will ensure every individual has an equal share in revenue utilization at all levels of administration.

Arthakranti Proposal

What is Arthakranti Proposal and who has given the proposal?

"Arthakranti Proposal" has been given by Pune (Maharashtra - India) based "Arthakranti Sansthan" which is an Economic Advisory body constituted by a group of Chartered Accountants and Engineers. This funda has been patented by the Sansthan.

Arthakranti Proposal is an effective and guaranteed solution for tackling Black Money Generation, Price Rise & Inflation, Corruption, Fiscal Deficit, Unemployment, Ransom and Funding for Terrorism. It is also a solution for increasing GDP & industrial growth and good governance.

What is in the Proposal?

Arthakranti Proposal has FIVE point of actions simultaneously.

1. Scrap all 56 Taxes including income tax.

2. Recall and scrap high denomination currencies of 1000, 500 and 100 rupees and 50 rupees. In case of the USA recall and scrap all currency notes higher than $5 or $10 *(Note: for the purposes of this book scrap all notes).*

3. All high value transactions *(for the purposes of this book all transactions)* to be made only through banking system like cheque, DD, online and electronic.

4. Fix limit on cash transaction and no taxing on cash transaction *(for the purposes of this book no cash transaction to be allowed).*

5. For government revenue collection introduce single point tax system through banking system – Banking Transaction Tax (2% to 0.7%) on only Credit Amount.

Important Points to note

1. As of today total banking transactions is more than 2.7 lakh crores *(1 lakh = 100 thousand and 1 crore = 10 million)* per day say more

than 800 lakh crores annually *(in case of USA it is hundreds and thousands of Billions Dollars)*.

2. Less than 20% transactions are made through banking system as of today and more than 80% transactions are made in cash only, which is not traceable.

3. One does not need to carry a lot of money to do one's normal daily shopping and with today's electronic money *(debit & credit cards)* one does not need to carry paper money.

What will happen if All FIFTY SIX Taxes (including income tax) are scrapped?

1. Salaried people will bring home more money which will increase purchasing power of the family.

2. All commodities including Petrol, Diesel, FMCG will become cheaper by 35% to 52%.

3. No question of Tax evasion, so no black money generation.

4. Business sector will get boosted. So will self employment.

What will happen if 2000 / 500 / 100 / 50 Rupees currency notes *(in case of the USA all $100 / $50 / $20 bills)* are recalled and scrapped?

1. Corruption through cash will be stopped 100%.

2. Black money will be either converted to white or will vanish as billions of 1000/500/100 / 50 currency notes *(in case of the USA all $100 / $50 / $20 bills)* hidden in bags without use will become simple pieces of paper having no value.

3. Unaccounted hidden huge cash is sky rocketing the prices of properties, land, houses, jewellery, etc. and hard earned money

is loosing its value; this trend will stop immediately.

4. Kidnapping and ransom, "Supari killing" will stop.

5. Terrorism supported by cash transaction will stop.

6. Cannot buy high value property in cash showing very less registry prices.

7. Circulation of "Fake Currency" will stop because fake currency printing for less value notes will not be viable *(for the purposes of this book, since paper money will cease to exist there will be no fake currency)*.

What will happen when Banking Transaction Tax (2% to 0.7%) is implemented?

1. As of today if BTT is implemented govt can fetch 800 x 2% = 16 lakh crore *(1 lakh = 100 thousand and 1 crore = 10 million)* whereas current taxing system is generating less than

59

14 lakh crore revenue *(1 lakh = 100 thousand and 1 crore = 10 million)*.

2. When 50% of total transaction will be covered by BTT, obtaining revenue of 2000 to 2500 lakh crores *(1 lakh = 100 thousand and 1 crore = 10 million)*, government will need to fix BTT as low as 1% to 0.7% and this will again boost banking transactions many fold.

3. No separate machinery like income tax department will be needed and tax amount will be directly deposited in state / central / district administration account immediately *(for the purposes of this book, tax amount will be directly deposited into the world administration account, which will be further distributed equally among the national, state, district, sub-district, town, constituency / locality administrations)*.

4. As transaction tax amount will be very less, public will prefer it instead of paying huge amount against prevailing FIFTY SIX direct / indirect taxes.

5. There will be no tax evasion and government will get huge revenue for development and employment generation.

6. For any special revenue for special projects, government can slightly raise BTT say from 1% to 1.2% and this 0.2% increase will generate 4,00,000 crores *(1 crore = 10 million)* additional funds.

Effect of it, if implemented today

1. Prices of all things will come down.

2. Salaried people will get more cash in hand.

3. Purchasing power of Society will increase.

4. Demand will get boosted, so will production and industrialization and ultimately more employment opportunity for youth.

5. Surplus revenue to the government for effective health/ education/ infrastructure/ security/ social.

The below text is not part of the Arthakranti Proposal but part of a new system of world government

A world bank set up by the world administration as mentioned in the previous chapter shall maintain virtual/electronic money balances of all individuals and entities and enable virtual money transactions through system of cheque/check books, debit cards, electronic money transfer and other such systems. The Banking Transaction Tax mentioned above will be automatically deducted or debited from the amount credited into an individual's or entity's bank account (*including his/her/its world bank account)* and transferred or credited to the world administration's account in the world bank.

Law & Rights In A Truly Democratic System Of World Government

Universal law and set of rights

Universal law

There shall be 1 universal law that shall apply to all citizens of the world equally.:

One shall not harm *(or his/her/its actions shall not lead to harming of)* another being either physically or mentally, except in self defence or self preservation or in protecting law & order and human rights, and that too as a last resort after all other options are exhausted or none available.

Cheating, stealing, burglary, robbery, defrauding will be considered as mentally harming another being. Also, creating noise and disturbing peace will also be considered as causing mental harm.

Teaching a subject that is neither a science, scientifically proven, historical fact, skill-set, form of

63

art or entertainment to a minor *(child below the age of 18)* in any form *(this includes teaching of the subject by parents & family as well)* will be considered as mentally harming the child, since it stunts the child's mental development and prevents him/her from thinking logically and with an open mind. This includes all religious subjects, texts, doctrines, practices, customs, etc.. It also includes making a child practice religious doctrines, customs, etc.. One can, however, teach religion to an adult *(once the child has reached 18 and he/she/it voluntarily wishes to learn the subject without undue force or any form of coercion)*. However, practising of religion is allowed in private by all. Public practice of religion is not allowed *(at least not in front of a minor or child below 18)*.

Saying, writing and displaying something that may offend another being is not considered as causing mental harm, since the other person has the option of not listening to, reading or seeing what is said, written or displayed. However, forcing someone to listen, read and see something he/she/it does not want to *(when he/she/it is not under contract to do so)* is considered as causing mental harm. Also, defaming a living being or his/her/its dead parents or dead grandparents with untrue facts which are not meant as a joke or form of satire will be considered as causing mental harm.

Forcing an individual to do anything that he/she/it does not want to and is not under contract to do so is considered as causing mental harm. Note: a person incarcerated automatically comes under contract of the administration that has incarcerated him/her/it as a way of paying off his/her/its debts to society for the harm and destruction that he/she/it caused.

Boycotting another being is not considered as causing mental harm, since the individual being boycotted has the option of fending for himself/herself or moving to another location where he/she will be wanted or taken care of.

Also, possession of a weapon by any individual other than a police officer on duty or officer of the special forces on duty will not be allowed or will be illegal *(this includes all guns, swords, etc. but excludes kitchen knives and other cutting tools used in industry, etc.).* Even a police officer is only entitled to a weapon that immobilizes from a distance and not one that can kill. And the officer must surrender the weapon when he/she is not on duty.

Universal rights

Every individual has the freedom to say, write, display or do anything as long as it does not violate the above universal law in any way.

Every individual has the freedom to move about anywhere unless he/she/it breaks a local law or the above universal law *(which leads to imprisonment)*.

Local laws

Apart from the above universal law & set of rights, every locality can have its own laws. However, these laws cannot contradict the above universal law & set of rights.

The Justice System And The Administering Of Justice

The Justice System

The Constituency/Locality Court of Justice

For minor disputes between 2 or more residents of a constituency, the matter can be brought in front of the constituency/locality committee (which will also act as a constituency/locality court of justice) for resolution.

The Town Court Of Justice

If a party is not satisfied with the verdict of the constituency/locality committee and for larger disputes or matters that involve 2 or more constituencies/localities within a town, the matter can be brought in front of (filed in) the Town court.

Every Town will have as many Town courts as ¼ number of constituencies/localities within it (this number can be increased or reduced as required/not required). The Town cabinet will have a justice ministry/department which will see to the administration of the Town courts and also recommend a list of judges who will be appointed by the Town assembly through majority vote. This list will be renewed every 6 months and presented to the Town assembly for appointment/re-appointment of judges.

The Town assembly along with the justice department/ministry will also frame rules regarding the time period within which various types of cases should be decided by the judges, failing which the judge/judges will be removed/replaced and punished with a fine and incarceration due to negligence of duty and causing mental harm to parties due to delay of justice.

The Sub-District Court Of Justice

If a party is not satisfied with the Town court's verdict and for matters involving 2 or more towns within a sub-district, the matter can be brought in front of (filed in) the Sub-district court.

Every Sub-district will have as many Sub-district courts as ¼ number of towns within it (this number can be increased or reduced as required/not required). The Sub-district cabinet will have a justice ministry/department which will see to the administration of the Sub-district courts and also recommend a list of judges who will be appointed by the Sub-district assembly through majority vote. This list will be renewed every 6 months and presented to the Sub-district assembly for appointment/re-appointment of judges.

The Sub-district assembly along with the justice department/ministry will also frame rules regarding the time period within which various types of cases should be decided by the judges, failing which the judge will be removed/replaced and punished with a fine and incarceration due to negligence of duty and causing mental harm to parties due to delay of justice.

The District Court Of Justice

If a party is not satisfied with the Sub-district court's verdict and for matters involving 2 or more sub-districts within a district, the matter can be brought in front of (filed in) the District court.

Every District will have as many District courts as ¼ number of sub-districts within it (this number can be increased or reduced as required/not required).

The District cabinet will have a justice ministry/department which will see to the administration of the District courts and also recommend a list of judges who will be appointed by the District assembly through majority vote. This list will be renewed every 6 months and presented to the District assembly for appointment/re-appointment of judges.

The District assembly along with the justice department/ministry will also frame rules regarding the time period within which various types of cases should be decided by the judges, failing which the judge will be removed/replaced and punished with a fine and incarceration due to negligence of duty and causing mental harm to parties due to delay of justice.

The State Court Of Justice

If a party is not satisfied with the District court's verdict and for matters involving 2 or more districts within a state, the matter can be brought in front of (filed in) the State court.

Every State will have as many State courts as ¼ number of districts within it (this number can be increased or reduced as required/not required). The

State cabinet will have a justice ministry/department which will see to the administration of the State courts and also recommend a list of judges who will be appointed by the State assembly through majority vote. This list will be renewed every 6 months and presented to the State assembly for appointment/re-appointment of judges.

The State assembly along with the justice department/ministry will also frame rules regarding the time period within which various types of cases should be decided by the judges, failing which the judge will be removed/replaced and punished with a fine and incarceration due to negligence of duty and causing mental harm to parties due to delay of justice.

The National Court Of Justice

If a party is not satisfied with the State court's verdict and for matters involving 2 or more states within a nation, the matter can be brought in front of (filed in) the National court.

Every Nation will have as many National courts as ¼ number of states within it (this number can be increased or reduced as required/not required). The

National cabinet will have a justice ministry/department which will see to the administration of the National courts and also recommend a list of judges who will be appointed by the National assembly through majority vote. This list will be renewed every 6 months and presented to the National assembly for appointment/re-appointment of judges.

The National assembly along with the justice department/ministry will also frame rules regarding the time period within which various types of cases should be decided by the judges, failing which the judge will be removed/replaced and punished with a fine and incarceration due to negligence of duty and causing mental harm to parties due to delay of justice.

The World Court Of Justice

If a party is not satisfied with the National court's verdict and for matters involving 2 or more Nations, the matter can be brought in front of (filed in) the World court.

There will be as many World courts as ¼ number of nations in the world (this number can be increased or reduced as required/not required). The World cabinet will have a justice ministry/department which will see to the administration of the World courts and also recommend a list of judges who will be appointed by the World assembly through majority vote. This list will be renewed every 6 months and presented to the World assembly for appointment/re-appointment of judges.

The World assembly along with the justice department/ministry will also frame rules regarding the time period within which various types of cases should be decided by the judges, failing which the judge will be removed/replaced and punished with a fine and incarceration due to negligence of duty and causing mental harm to parties due to delay of justice.

Note: A party may directly approach a higher court or even the highest court (which is the World court) for justice, if that party feels it is not going to get justice in the lower courts. However since the higher court's verdict holds precedence over a lower court, once the party approaches the highest court, it will have no other recourse but to abide by the court's verdict/decision.

The Administering of justice

While administering justice every being shall be treated equally and as an individual. There will be no grouping or categorization of individuals while administering justice. Every person/being shall be treated as an individual of independent mind and equal status under the justice system.

Every party will fight it's own case in the courts. However if required the court will provide a consultant to assist the party. There will be no lawyers. On request the court may even appoint an investigator to uncover further missing information and this information will be provided to all those present in court and cannot be withheld from either parties or the judge/judges.

All court proceedings will be video recorded and transcribed. The court video recordings and transcripts will be made available to all the parties in the case and all those present in court for current and future reference.

For all criminal cases the prosecuting party or public prosecutor will be the chief of police or chief investigator responsible for investigating the case.

If the matter concerns the larger public interest then media persons will be allowed to record and broadcast the proceedings in absolute silence. However they won't be allowed to interrogate any of the parties or members of the court attending to the case.

Depending on the seriousness of the case and the impact it has on the parties concerned as well as on the general public, every trial will have 3 or 5 or 7 judges presiding over a trial or case and the verdict needs to be unanimous or have majority consensus from the judges after due deliberation among themselves. In case of small cases there can be only 1 judge presiding over the trial or case.

The judge/judges for each trial will be picked randomly by a tamper proof computer system and a judge will be randomly assigned to a trial in any of the courts within that jurisdiction. (eg. a town court judge will be randomly assigned a trial in any of the town courts within the town, a sub-district court judge will be randomly assigned a trial in any of the

Sub-District courts within the Sub-District, a District court judge will be randomly assigned a trial in any of the District courts within the District, a state court judge will be randomly assigned a trial in any of the state courts within the state, a national court judge will be randomly assigned a trial in any of the national courts within the nation, a world court judge will be randomly assigned a trial in any of the world courts).

There will be no capital punishment or medieval form of punishment such as cutting off of arms, etc., since every individual has unique skills that can be used for the benefit of people at large, and even if an individual does not possess skills he/she/it can be used in constructive work for the benefit of people at large *(an individual who is incarcerated automatically enters into contract with the administration to be utilized in any constructive occupation that benefits society as a way of repaying his/her/its debts to society for the harm and destruction caused by him/her/it)*. Also, every individual has the potential for good and can be rehabilitated.

Note:

If fresh evidence is uncovered after a verdict has been given, the case/trial can be re-opened and verdict changed.

Enforcement Of Law & Order And Protecting The World

Security and police forces

Constituency/locality police

Every constituency/locality will have its own security or police force to deal with security and crimes & investigations within the constituency/locality.

Town police

Every town will have its own police force. The town police will deal with security and crimes & investigations involving 2 or more constituencies/localities within the town. The police of a constituency/locality may also take the help of the town police to deal with security and crimes & investigations within the constituency/locality.

Sub-district police

Every sub-district will have its own police force. The sub-district police will deal with security and crimes

& investigations involving 2 or more towns within the sub-district. The police of a town may also take the help of the sub-district police to deal with security and crimes & investigations within the town.

District police

Every district will have its own police force. The district police will deal with security and crimes & investigations involving 2 or more sub-districts within the district. The police of a sub-district may also take the help of the district police to deal with security and crimes & investigations within the sub-district.

State police

Every state will have its own police force. The state police will deal with security and crimes & investigations involving 2 or more districts within the state. The police of a district may also take the help of the state police to deal with security and crimes & investigations within the district.

National police

Every nation will have its own police force. The national police will deal with security and crimes &

investigations involving 2 or more states within the nation. The police of a state may also take the help of the national police to deal with security and crimes & investigations within the state.

World police

There will also be a world police which will deal with security and crimes & investigations involving 2 or more nations of the world. The police of a nation may also take the help of the world police to deal with security and crimes & investigations within the nation.

Special forces

Other than the regular police forces as mentioned above there will also be a world Special Forces whose job will be to protect the integrity and sanctity of the system of world government as stated in this book.

The Special Forces will consist of 8 to 10 small Battalions which will comprise of equal number of personnel randomly chosen from all the National Police forces and the World Police force equally ie. all the National Police forces and the World Police force will contribute an equal number of personnel (which will be randomly chosen through a computer system) to the Special Forces. Half of the Special Forces personnel will serve a 3 month term and Half will serve a 4 month term after which they will be replaced through a similar procedure of randomly selected personnel from all the National Police forces and World Police force equally. The random selection of personnel will be done through a computer system whereby no personnel will repeat tenure for the next 2 years. After their tenure is up the personnel will go back to their duties within their respective Police forces. The personnel selected from all the National Police forces and the World Police force for the Special Forces will be randomly put into any one of the 8 to 10 battalions of the force. The commander of one of the battalions will be randomly selected from the commanding officers of the World Police. For the commanders of the remaining 7 to 9 battalions 1 commander each will be randomly selected from 7 to 9 randomly chosen National Police forces ie. 1 commander chosen from each of the 7 to 9 randomly chosen Nation's Police force. The commanders of half the number of battalions (4 or 5 battalions) will serve a 3 month term and half will serve a 4 month term after which they will be replaced through a similar system of randomly chosen commanders. The random selection of both the commanders and the nations will be done through a computer system, such that no commander will repeat tenure for another 2 to 3 years.

There will be a Special Forces Action Committee consisting of 2 randomly chosen world court judges through a computer system and 8 randomly chosen national court judges from 8 different randomly chosen nations again through a computer system giving this committee a total of 10 members. The tenure of the members of this committee will be 3 months after which all the members will be once again replaced by a new set of members consisting of 2 randomly chosen world court judges and 8 randomly chosen National Court judges from 8 different randomly chosen nations again through a computer system which also makes sure a Special Forces Action Committee member does not repeat tenure for another 2 to 3 years. The judges chosen to be members of the Special Forces Action Committee will be absolved of their duties as judge during their tenure as members in this committee. The job of this committee will be to monitor world events for any threat to the integrity and sanctity of the System of World Government as stated in this book and promptly call the Special Forces into action to take care of the threat. A minimum of 6 members of this committee will need to come to an agreement to sanction any action by the Special Forces. The following will be considered a threat to the Integrity and Sanctity of the System of World Government as stated in this book:

1) The World president or any minister in the World Cabinet refuses to step down when they are replaced by the World Assembly. Whenever the world president or any minister of the World cabinet is replaced by the World Assembly the Special Forces Action Committee and all The Special Forces officers will be notified about the same and the Special Forces Personnel will immediately escort the replaced President or the replaced minister out of office and if he/she resists or refuses to be escorted out of office, he/she will be immediately arrested.

2) A National Cabinet Minister or National president refuses to step down when replaced and the Nation's Security Force or the World Security Force is unable to or do not take care of the situation.

3) The World Assembly, any National Assembly, any State Assembly, any District Assembly, any Sub-District Assembly and any Town-Assembly stops functioning in the manner as laid down in this book where by a representative stops obeying the instructions of the people who appoint them, stops relaying information to the people who appoint them and refuses to step down when replaced and the respective regular security forces are unable to take care and correct the situation.

4) If the World Administration or Police interferes in the administration or policing of a nation. Any National Administration or Police interferes in the administration or policing of a state within it. Any State Administration or Police interferes in the administration or policing of a District within it. Any District Administration or Police interferes in the administration or policing of a Sub-District within it. Any Sub-District Administration or Police interferes in the administration or policing of a Town within it. Any Town Administration or Police interferes

in the administration or policing of a constituency/locality within it.

5) If the World Assembly, or any National Assembly or any State Assembly or any District Assembly or any Sub-District Assembly or any Town Assembly or any Constituency/Locality enacts a law that contradicts the Universal Law and Universal Rights as stated in this book.

6) If any person who is not an officer of a police/security force on active duty comes to possess any weapon.

7) If it is detected that a person or group of persons are rebelling or planning to rebel against any aspect of the system of World Government as stated in this book.

The Special Forces Action Committee members will be sworn to secrecy and their identity will only be known to the Officers of the Special Forces. After the 3 month tenure of the Special Forces Action Committee members is up the members will be escorted out of office by the personnel of Special Forces to be replaced by a new set of randomly selected members as mentioned above. The list of newly selected members of the Committee will be provided to the commanding officers of the Special Forces every 3 months. Every citizen of the world will have a means to contact the Special Forces Action Committee via email or other electronic means (without knowing the identity of the members) if he/she detects a threat to the integrity or sanctity of the System of World Government as stated in this book and as per the list of threats mentioned above.

Special Division to Protect Against External Threat

There will also be another division set up to protect the world from an external threat not of this world such as rogue Asteroids, Comets, etc.. A separate ministry will be created to see to the functioning of this Special Division. Any action undertaken by the this Special Division will require sanction or need to be endorsed by the World assembly.

Use of weapons and their manufacture

All weapons will be banned *(including guns and swords but excluding kitchen knives and other cutting tools used in industry, etc.).* However, the police forces will be armed with special weapons that can immobilize individuals from a distance without harming them seriously. The officers in these police forces will only be allowed access to these weapons when on duty. They will have to surrender the weapons which shall be kept under special lock & key when off duty.

The special forces whose job is to protect the integrity and sanctity of the System of World Government as stated in this book will have access to special weapons that can immobilize people on a very large scale for a longer duration without causing serious harm. Any action taken by them will require sanction from majority members of the Special Forces Action Committee (minimum 6 members out of 10) and it will also be the function of Special Forces Personnel to escort the replaced World President or World Cabinet Minister out of Office as well as escort the Special Forces Action Committee members out of office once their 3 month tenure is over. The officers in the special forces shall only have access to their weapons when on duty. They shall have to surrender their weapons which shall be kept under special lock & key when off duty.

A special body will be set up for developing and manufacturing the weapons used by the police and special forces as mentioned above.

The Special Division whose job is to protect the world from external threats will work on R&D and developing systems to protect the planet from threats from outer space such as rogue Asteroids, Comets, etc.. Any action or development undertaken by this division will require sanction or endorsement by the World Assembly.

All other weapons and sources to manufacture them will be abolished and destroyed, so that no one can get hold of them. The technology for manufacturing some of the destructive weapons and a few weapons to be used in case of very grave emergency as a last resort, shall be kept under special lock and key and their usage will require the sanction of the world assembly, world cabinet of ministers as well as the president. A system will be developed such that access to and usage of these weapons will not be allowed or possible without a special system of consent from the majority members of the world assembly as well as the consent from the world cabinet of ministers and the world president.

Law Governing Land Ownership

World administration in charge of all land and division of land among various administrative units

Since land is not created by man, all land shall be owned by the world administration. This land shall be divided among the nations based on the land occupied by the residents of the nation. The land parcel of every nation shall be divided among its states based on land occupied by residents of each state. The land parcel of every state shall be divided among its districts based on land occupied by residents of each district. The land parcel of every district shall be divided among its sub-districts based on land occupied by residents of each sub-district. The land parcel of every sub-district shall be divided among its towns based on land occupied by residents of each town. The land parcel of every town shall be divided among its constituencies/localities based on the land occupied by residents of each constituency/locality.

Leasing of land

All land shall be considered leased to existing owners, whether individuals or organizations, for a period of 30 to 40 years *(except for land owned by government entities, which will either belong to the world administration or the administration of the nation or state or district or sub-district or town or constituency/locality on which the land lies)*. No piece of land can be leased to an individual or organization for a period greater than 30 to 40 years.

After the expiry of a lease, the lease for the piece of land for the next 30 to 40 years is immediately auctioned and the lease will go to the highest bidder irrespective of the community or region the bidder *(individual or organization)* belongs to.

50 to 60% of increase in the lease price or lease value of the land *(from the original price paid by the last owner)* will go to the previous or last lease owner.

The last owner of the lease may re-purchase the lease of the land by outbidding the other bidders and he/she/it will only have to pay the original price

+ 40 to 50% of the increase in price or value, since he/she/it gets 50 to 60% of increase in value of the lease.

Only the land is leased and not any building that lies on it. The building will belong to the individual or organization who built it or purchased it. The new lease owner cannot occupy the building or cause destruction to it in any way without the explicit permission from the owner/s of the building. However, he/she/it does have the right to charge rent for the building occupying his/her/its land. If the owner/s of the building is/are unable to pay the rent, they have to move the building elsewhere. Alternatively the new land owner can outright purchase the building or the building owner/s can sell it to him/her/it.

The owner of the land lease may further lease all or part of the land to another individual or organization for a period not more than the remaining duration of his/her/its lease.

Acquiring land for government use

Land can be acquired for public works such as roads, pipelines, etc. or for nature reserves, etc. from existing lease owners by the locality / town / sub-district / district / state / national / world administration. Whenever such land is acquired, the last lease owner shall get 50 to 60% of the increase in market value *(from the original/last price paid by last owner and the current market price correctly determined through a formula based on latest bids for surrounding land, soil quality, etc.)* in addition to the original price for the remainder of his/her/its lease period.

Administration responsible for auctioning land lease

The responsibility for auctioning the land will fall on the administration of the constituency or locality on which the land lies. If the piece of land lies between 2 or more constituencies or localities, then the responsibility will fall on the administration of the town on which it lies. If the piece of land lies between 2 or more towns, then the responsibility falls on the administration of the sub-district on which the land lies. If the land lies between 2 or more sub-districts, then the responsibility falls on the administration of the district on which the land lies. If the land lies between 2 or more districts, then the responsibility falls on the administration of the state on which the land lies. If the land lies between 2 or more states, then the responsibility falls on the administration of the nation on which the land lies. If the land lies between 2 or more nations, then the responsibility falls on the world administration.

Distribution of revenue from lease of land

From the total revenue collected from the lease of land 20% to 30% of the revenue collected through the leasing of land will go to the world administration and the remaining 70% to 80% will be divided equally among all the nations *(the system of revenue division will be automated, i.e. 20% to 30% will be credited into the world administration's account and the remaining will be credited to the accounts of all the nations equally).*

70% to 80% of a nation's share of revenue from lease of land will be divided equally among the states of the nation *(this will be automated - from the revenue credited to the nation's account 70% to 80% will be automatically debited and credited into the accounts of all states within the nation equally).*

70% to 80% of a state's share of revenue from lease of land will be divided equally among the districts of the state *(this will be automated - from the revenue credited to the state's account 70% to 80% will be automatically debited and credited into the accounts of all districts within the state equally).*

70% to 80% of a district's share of revenue from lease of land will be divided equally among the sub-districts of the district *(this will be automated - from the revenue credited to the district's account 70% to 80% will be automatically debited and credited into the accounts of all Sub-districts within the district equally).*

70% to 80% of a Sub-district's share of revenue from lease of land will be divided equally among the towns of the sub-district *(this will be automated - from the revenue credited to the sub-district's account 70% to 80% will be automatically debited and credited into the accounts of all towns within the sub-district equally).*

70% to 80% of a town's share of revenue from lease of land will be divided equally among the constituencies/localities of the town *(this will be automated - from the revenue credited to the town's account 70% to 80% will be automatically debited and credited into the accounts of all constituencies/localities within the town equally).*

Law Governing Corporates

All corporations shall be registered under a body set up by the world administration. They will also all have an account with the world bank in addition to their existing bank accounts which can be used for cash or banking transactions.

The laws governing corporate entities will remain pretty much the same as the corporate laws prevailing in most countries today.

However, to make the board of directors more responsible or accountable, there will exist one additional law, and that will be as follows:

The board of directors will be directly liable for any debt incurred by the corporation during their tenure as directors, which the corporation is unable to pay off. They will also be liable for any debts incurred due to decisions taken while they were/are directors.

Conclusion

The government should be the servant of the people, and not the people slaves of the government. The government is formed or appointed or elected to serve the people and not vice versa. The government cannot control the people, it is the people who control the government. If the Government controls the people, then it is Dictatorship. You cannot have dictatorship in the name of democracy, whether it is for 1 day or for a number of years. The stress should be on Government For The People, By The People. The People Should Control the government and Not Vice Versa. It is the People who make the world. Therefore nothing can be above the people.

The citizens are the most powerful. Even religion cannot be above the citizen. Religion is man made. It was made by man to bring order to chaos in Ancient Times. A wise person framed some principles to be followed in order for people to live in harmony. Since people would not take his/her words at face value, he/she had to say that these were told to him/her by a/the Supreme Being or God. And this was misconstrued as religion or word of God. If there is a God or Supreme Being, he will help one & all, and God won't demand worship. It is only man that demands worship. By worshipping God you are only bringing him down to the level of man. God does not want any customs or rituals to be followed, only man does. God only wants everyone to live in harmony & that is all. He doesn't even want man to believe in him. He is so great that he will help one & all. Remember God will not tell one thing to one person (a person belonging to one religion) & something else to another (a person belonging to another religion). Only man does this. You don't have to take my word or any other person's word on this just listen to your inner self. Make your own judgement through your own experiences in life. You should be able to find this out for yourself. After all only you know what is best for you. No one can tell you that. Use your own common sense. You should not be influenced by what you read or hear. You should learn from your own experiences. Nothing can teach you better than that.